REPTILES AND AMPHIBIANS

STERLING

GET CHARMED BY **REPTILES AND AMPHIBIANS** while you explore...

WHAT ARE REPTILES?

It might not be Halloween. And yet reptiles can look scary. But that's just because all reptiles are covered with dry scales and not hair or feathers (Imagine a feathery reptile!). Also, they breathe air and have a backbone.

Blow Hot, Blow Cold

Reptiles are cold-blooded creatures. That means that if it's hot outside, then the temperature of their bodies will be hot. If it is cold outside, their bodies will be cold. Whereas we mammals are warm-blooded, which means we can control our body temperature.

Basking and Brumation

One can find reptiles sunbathing and they don't do this for a tan, but to keep their bodies warm. This is called basking.

If they're cold, they get lazy and aren't able to move quickly then. So, when temperatures drop, reptiles get very lethargic to save energy. This is when they hibernate (called brumation in case of reptiles). But unlike mammals, they don't actually sleep or live off reserves of fat.

A Basking Crocodile

We're Really Old

Fossils of reptiles have been found that are more than 300 million years old! They ruled life on land for more than 150 million years and birds and mammals are their descendants.

Turning Over a New Leaf

Reptiles shed their scales and replace them throughout their life. Most of them shed their scales one by one or in patches but snakes shed all of them at one go.

A snake's skin being shed

Born with a Tooth

All reptile babies have an egg tooth which sharply juts out from their snouts. This is there so that they can cut through the thick shells of their eggs to come out into the world.

Coming Through...

Reptiles have some very interesting ways of finding their way around the world. Snakes and some lizards push the scales of their bellies against the ground to get a grip and then pull their bodies so that they can move forward. Sea turtles swim with the help of flippers or webbed feet and alligators and crocodiles move through water by lashing their tails. And even though no known reptile can fly, there are only a few snakes and lizards that can glide across the air. Fortunately!

REPTILE MYTHS

Dragon Power

Whether fire-breathing or not fire-breathing, the dragons of myth have usually been shown as reptiles—they hatch from eggs and have scaly bodies. Europeans showed dragons with bat-like wings who are mostly evil whereas Chinese dragons do look like huge snakes but are forces of good.

The Evil Serpent

In Jewish and Christian traditions, it is held that it was a snake who misled the first humans, Adam and Eve and that is how evil came into the world. And so the snake was cursed to crawl on its belly in shame.

Early Christians disliked the snake so much that there is a famous story in which it is said that St. Patrick drove out all the snakes from Ireland with his staff and that is why there are no snakes in Ireland! Try figuring out the real reason yourself and see what you come up with.

On the Back of the Turtle

A lot of ancient myths thought the turtle to stand for stability. There are legends in places as far apart as India, Japan and North America that the earth was supported on the back of a turtle with nothing else to support it. And one still wonders who might have supported the turtle?

TUATARA

It looks like a lizard but is not actually one. The tuatara is found only on around 32 islands off the coast of New Zealand. They've survived on these islands because there are no rats there who like to eat these reptiles. This is because New Zealand split away from the major landmass a long time back and separated from rats too.

As of now, not even people are allowed on them (if people come, rats will join). Anyway, these islands are surrounded by huge cliffs which makes it tough for ships to land.

A Long Egg-spectation

A tuatara stays in its egg for fifteen months before it hatches. This is the longest any reptile stays in its egg.

If Music be the Food...

These music-lovers can actually come out of their holes to hear someone singing. They like solos but they prefer a rousing chorus and are more likely to come out during that!

Ooh Spikey!

They have sharp and bony spikes along their backs, just like dinosaurs. They've been around for 240 million years and are survivors from the age of dinosaurs and that's why, they're called 'living fossils'.

MEET THE LIZARDS

Six-lined Racerunner

Speed Demons

Most lizards have strong muscular legs and can travel really fast. The racerunner maybe short and only 8 to 16 inches long, but can run as fast as 24 km per hour. Not only that, the fastest lizard in the world is the Black Spiny-tailed Iguana which grows upto 5 feet for males and 3 feet for females and can run as fast as 34.9 km per hour!

A Lucky Break

Many species of lizard have tails that break off when touched. These broken tails wriggle even then, which distracts the predator. This lizard now takes advantage of this opportunity to escape. And yes, the tail grows back!

LIZARD PROFILES

Green Basilisk Lizard

To escape from danger it can run on water without sinking for as long as 15 feet! After that, being a very good swimmer, it can quickly go underwater and remain there for 30 minutes.
Not only that, this dandy lizard has a high crest on its head and back to charm the ladies.

A Gecko's Grip

Geckos can climb the most slippery surfaces, even glass windows! This is because their feet have sticky plates under which are millions of really tiny hairs which help it to cling firmly.

The Little Webbed Wonder

The webbed feet gecko is at home in the reddish sands of the Namib Desert. Its webbed feet help it glide across the sand quickly and bury itself in it and its colour helps it camouflage itself.

A Brave Coward?

The frilled lizard is quite an amusing creature. When it feels threatened, it opens its mouth, spreads its flaps and hisses fiercely. And yet, if the attacker doesn't go anywhere, the lizard simply does an about turn and flees for dear life.

Take Cover...

Draco lizards have folds which are extensions of their ribs. They take these out, spread them and fly, gliding as far as thirty feet. This is done to escape predators, find food and to get mates.

Smart Guys

They're fast and quick tongued. Not witty, of course, but they have a tongue that's 50 centimeters long which they flick in the blink of an eye to gobble up their prey.

Scary huh!

The green anole lizard has a throat sac that is enlarged (called a 'dewlap') and brightly coloured. In order to defend its te rritory, it blows up the dewlap to scare males anoles or other animals away.

A Living 'Dragon'

The largest and heaviest of the lizards, reaching around 10 feet and more than 136 kilos (300 pounds), Komodo Dragons can eat water buffalos and have been known to eat even humans. Their saliva is poisonous because around 50 strains of bacteria live there. Once they've bitten a prey, they can follow it for days till the poison works.

Colour for a Cause

The lizards that are famous because they can change the colour of their skin are known as chameleons.

A lot of people think that chameleons change colour to match their surroundings. But that's not true. They do it to show their reactions and emotions or under the influence of the surrounding light and temperature.

Welcome to Madagascar

Half the species of chameleons in the world live on the island of Madagascar itself! What an island!

A Sticky Customer

The chameleon lies still, waiting for a juicy fly to buzz past it. The moment it appears, it shoots out its tongue, which is long and sticky, and pulls it back to munch on its meal.

WHAT'S UP, CROC? CROCODILE FACTS

We're Survivors

We have survived from the age of dinosaurs and have been around for about 80 million years.

Crocodiles vs Alligators

Crocodiles	Alligators
Have a narrow V-shaped snouts.	Have a flatter, wider head, which means that their noses are U-shaped.
A crocodile has a large tooth in its lower jaw which shows when its mouth is closed.	For them, this tooth doesn't show.
Crocodiles are more aggressive	They tend to avoid danger.

Chinese Alligator

Unlikely Cousins

You might think that crocodiles are more closely related to other reptiles, but interestingly, their closest relatives are birds.

There are only two species of alligators in the world- the American alligator and the Chinese alligator. The Chinese alligator is almost extinct.

Stomach this!

A crocodile has a very powerful digestive system. It doesn't have grinding teeth, but it can digest all the shells and bones that it eats because alligators and crocodiles have rocks in their tummies called gastroliths that help in digestion. All this is the more surprising because their stomachs are not bigger than our heads!

Crocablanca...or a Crocodile Romance

In their more romantic moods, male crocodiles hum a low tone that can only be detected by a female crocodile, even if she is miles away. When they're together, the male gently rubs the female's snout and blows bubbles underneath her, which release crocodile perfume.

A Gentle Giant?

The ferocious Nile crocodile, also the second largest crocodile, can eat up to half its body weight. But beneath that hard exterior there perhaps lies a soft heart. It softly rolls its eggs in its mouth to help them to hatch (rather than going snap!).

In another example of its gentleness, it has struck a deal (called a symbiotic relationship) with some birds like the Egyptian Plover. The huge crocodile gets rid of blood sucking leeches by opening its mouth wide and allowing the bird to pick them. And so, the bird too benefits by having its meal in the process.

American Alligator

Around 150 million years old, it is a direct survivor from the age of dinosaurs who became extinct 65 million years ago.

Phew!

They were about to become extinct recently, but measures to ensure their protection have made them recover to a population of more than one million.

The Pot at the End of the Nose

Gharials or gavials have a long snout at the end of which there is a bulbous growth which is called a ghara, the Hindi word for "pot". It called so since it resembles a pot and is used to attract females and also to blow bubbles during courtship.

And The Prizes Go To...

For the Largest Reptile in the World

The Australian saltwater crocodile for growing as long as 23 feet. This one is dangerous, because it is also the most likely crocodile to eat a human.

For the Smallest Croc

The African dwarf crocodile, for hardly growing longer than 5 feet. Cute croc? Perhaps.

Spectacled Caiman

This is the most common of all crocodilians (that's what the whole group is called which includes crocodiles, alligators, gharials and caimans) . That is because they can adapt to both freshwater and salt water. In winter, they have a special pigment in their skin that turns their colour to a darker shade.

SNAKES: A BRIEF ENCOUNTER

Snakes are meat-eating reptiles with bodies that are long and slender, with no legs, no eyelids, no external ears and with broad scales on their bellies to move forward. They also have the familiar forked tongues that flick forward.

Just Looking Around

Snakes find their way around the world and hunt for prey by using their eyes or they can sense vibrations with their bodies. They can flick their tongues to pick up scents from the air to locate things around them. Pit vipers have pits on their heads to sense heat and boas and pythons have them on their lips.

Try swallowing a pumpkin and you'll appreciate the fact that snakes can swallow things that are up to 20 percent the size of their bodies. This is because its lower jaw is very flexible because its two halves are not tightly attached and so are the joints in its skull.

Ready? Charge!

Snakes can strike or lunge forward to get hold of their prey very fast. Some swallow small animals immediately, others like pythons grip their prey tightly and coil around them till they suffocate, while others inject venom to make them die or to paralyse them. The good news is that only one third of the total snake population is poisonous and people do not often die from snakebites.

Python

Keeping a Snake as a Pet

A lot of people are interested in snakes as pets. If you want to start, then having a Corn Snake is a good way because you can handle and care for it easily and it is non-poisonous.

Inland Taipan

Which country has the most number of poisonous snakes in the world?

Australia is home to nine out of ten of the world's most poisonous snakes, the most venomous of which is the Inland Taipan which can kill a full grown adult in two minutes.

Anaconda

Record Breakers

-The smallest snakes in the world are the blind snakes which are only around 8 inches long.

-The longest snake in the world is the reticulated python which can reach more than 26 feet in length, while the heaviest being the giant anaconda.

-The longest poisonous snake is the king cobra which reaches a length of around seventeen and a half feet.

The Bluffmaster

The Hognose snake, even though it is a non-poisonous snake, knows how to bluff its way out of danger. It'll act as if it is a venomous snake, flatten its head, hiss and strike but not bite. If the attacker calls off its bluff, it'll flip on to its back, writhe and bleed from its mouth and act as if it is dead, making itself unappetising to its predator.

Eastern Hog-nosed Snake

A Rattling Snake

A rattlesnake's 'rattle' is made up of keratin, the same pigment that makes up our skin and nails. A new segment is added to the rest of the segments when it sheds its skin. When these segments vibrate against each other, the rattling sound is heard.

King Cobras

- King Cobras can be 18 feet long—longest of all poisonous snakes.

- When attacked they can raise one third of their bodies and still thrust forward to attack.

- They are the only snakes that build nests for their eggs and they guard it till their babies hatch.

- The ideal snakes for snake charmers. Although they can hear, they can't hear sounds in their immediate surroundings. And they sway to the shape and the way the flute moves, rather than to its sound.

- The poison in a single bite can kill 20 people or an elephant! But don't worry, they like keeping to themselves and are only hostile if someone attacks them.

TURTLE TRAITS

Ye Olde Gentlemen

A lot of turtles can live longer than a hundred years. Adwaita, an Adabra Giant tortoise was the oldest known tortoise who died in Alipore Zoo, Kolkata, India in 2006 at the age of 255 years. Imagine, a tortoise who lived through all those drastic events in the world that happened in this time!

Galapagos Giant Tortoise

What's the difference between a Turtle and a Tortoise?

A tortoise is a turtle but not all turtles are tortoises. You can point out a tortoise if you see that:

- It's vegetarian (herbivorous).
- It's hidden-necked.
- It has a bigger and higher shell which is more domelike.
- It moves very slowly.
- Does not have webbed feet which other turtles have.

A Teeny Turtle

The smallest turtle in the world is a tortoise called the Speckled Padloper tortoise found in South Africa. It can grow only as long as 3 inches and be as light as 5 ounces, that is, 142 grams.

A group of turtles is called a bale. A bundle of straw bound tightly is also called a bale. Is there a connection?

Saving their Necks

Many turtles can tuck in their heads, legs and tails into their shells for protection. Turtles are separated into two groups based on the way they hide their necks. Those who take them back into their spine are called Cryptodira or Hidden-necked turtles. But those who turn the neck to one side and hide it under their shell are called Pleurodira or Side-necked turtles. Their necks are longer and their shells flatter. The top part of the shell of a turtle is called the carapace while the bottom part is called the plastron. It is made up of 60 connected bones and have nerve endings too. That is why the shell of a turtle can feel your finger if you touch it.

Hidden-necked Turtle

Side-necked Turtle

Heavy Duty Shells

The shell of a box turtle is so strong that it can bear a weight that is 200 times heavier than the turtle.

Is it a Boy?...Or is it a Girl?

It takes two months for turtle eggs to hatch and whether it's a boy or a girl, it depends on the temperature. So if it's below 29 degrees Celsius, it's a boy, if it's above that, it's a girl!

No matter how hard it tries, a turtle can't leave its shell.

A FEW TURTLE FRIENDS

Loggerhead Turtle

Loggerhead turtles are called so because they have large heads that look like big logs. They have strong jaws too which they use to crush animals with hard shells.

Childhood Memories

Very often, female loggerhead turtles swim back thousands of miles to the beach where she herself hatched to lay her eggs.

Green Sea Turtle

The green sea turtle has flippers that look like paddles which make them excellent swimmers.

Leatherback Turtle

It is the world's largest turtle, can be more than six and a half feet long and can weigh more than a ton!

Funny Food

Hawksbill turtles find highly poisonous sea sponges yummy, something that most animals can't afford to eat. Strange diet, isn't it?

Snap and Sway the Turtle Way

The alligator snapping turtle looks like a rock and has a tongue that looks like a juicy worm. It happily sits at the bottom of a pond, waving its tongue with its mouth open. When an unsuspecting fish comes by, snap goes its mouth. A clever customer, eh?

Ugh!

The Musk turtle is also known as Stinkpot. If irritated, it gives out a stinky yellowish fluid.

AMPHIBIANS

Types of Amphibians

There are three types of amphibians—frogs and toads, salamanders and newts and caecilians.

What makes them special

- Have four legs
- Have moist and slimy or dry and warty skin
- Live near water.
- They differ from reptiles because their skins don't have scales and most of them go back to water to breed.

Frogs and Toads

- Bodies without necks.
- Have strong hind legs with which they leap.
- They swim with webbed feet.
- Have long tongues which are sticky with which they catch food.
- Lots of species found—around 3800.

Caecilians

- Their skin is smooth.
- They burrow like earthworms.
- Their jaws have teeth.
- Lesser number of species—around 75.

Salamanders and Newts

- Limbs weaker than frogs.
- Have a tail.
- Skin is smooth and moist with which they breathe oxygen.
- They have a neck.
- Average number of species—around 340.

Yellow Spotted Salamander

FROGS AND TOADS

A Frog's View

- My hind legs are long.
- I have smooth and moist skin.
- I like water and I like spending time in it.
- I leap.
- My upper jaw has teeth.
- My ears or tympanum are larger than a toad's.
- I have webbed feet.

A Toad's View

- My hind legs are short.
- My skin is rough and warty but I have other good qualities, you know.
- Water isn't my favourite hideout. So I don't spend a lot of time there
- My hops are short when I walk.
- I don't have teeth.
- You heard it from the braggart. Do I have to say that my ears are smaller?
- My hind feet are webless.

Cane Toad

The Well-Trodden Path

If you take a frog or toad away from their territory, they'll smell and use the position of the stars to find their way back. And a lot of species manage to come back every year wherever they are to the same breeding grounds.

LIFE CYCLE OF A FROG

1. A frog lays a bunch of her eggs (called a spawn) in water.
2. After hatching, the little frogs are known as tadpoles. They live in water, have a tail with which they swim and breathe through gills.

   Tadpoles who are very young, feed on the yoke of their egg which is still in their gut.
3. After a few weeks, their hind legs grow out and then their front ones.

   At that time, they also eat insects and plants.
4. In the next stage, tadpoles become froglets. They start breathing with lungs, the legs are grown but there is still a bit of the tail left.
5. Of course, next stop is land.

   As a full grown adult.

Lost in the Frog

The Amazon River alone has 1000 out of the 5000 species of frog. It's really froggy out there, isn't it?

Croak-a-doodle-doo!

The male Spring Peeper announces the arrival of spring by making sounds like sleigh-bells in a chorus.

The American Bullfrog's deep and loud sound is like the mooing of a cow and that explains why "bull" is included in its name. And yes, it can be heard a quarter of a mile away!

The Carpenter frog sounds like the hammering of nails by a carpenter.

Barking tree frogs bark like a pack of dogs who've gone on a hunt.

Spring Peeper

American Bullfrog

You Poisonous Toad...er...Frog!

The poison dart frog, who is only the size of a paper clip, is both beautiful and dangerous. The beautiful colours and venom are there to scare predators away. It is one of the most poisonous animals in the world and the venom in a golden poison dart frog is enough to kill 10 people. The Embera people of Colombia have tipped their darts with this poison for centuries for hunting.

The Best Offence is a Fashionable Defence

When it encounters a threat, the Oriental Fire-Bellied Toad stands up or sometimes topples over to show its bright belly with black spots. And because it is not bluffing, it even secretes a poison after this. To add to its fashion sense, its eyes have triangular pupils.

Don't Try This At Home

Wallace's Flying Frog, also known as parachute frogs, leap from branches, spread out their webbed feet and with the help of the webbing between their toes and spread skin flaps, can glide as far as 50 feet. Their large toe pads help them land softly or to stick to trees.

Shock Value

The red-eyed tree frog loves to shock its predators. When it feels threatened, it flashes its bright red eyes and uses its bright skin to confuse and dazzle the predator. This gives the frog time to make its escape to safety.

SALAMANDERS

Female fire salamander about to be a mum.

Salamanders have bodies that are slender, long tails and a short nose. Like lizards they can grow back lost body parts, but unlike them, have no claws. Most of them have four toes in their front limbs and five at the back.

Barking Salamanders

Mudpuppies, also called waterdogs, as their name suggests, are the only salamanders who make a squeaky sound that reminds one of a dog's bark. You can make out a mudpuppy by the fact that it lives all its life underwater and by its red bushy gills which are on the outside. They grow up to be quite long for salamanders, averaging around 11 inches.

Mums with a Mission

The females of some species of salamanders are excellent mothers. They have been seen to curl up around their eggs to help them retain moisture in their shells. They also nudge their eggs to keep the inner membranes from sticking. Predators ought to be careful, for salamander mothers come to the defense of their eggs.

Female salamanders also have a way of identifying their own eggs if they're mixed up with others. This mechanism is in them most probably to stop them from eating their own eggs.

The Child Who Never Wanted to Grow Up

The axolotl salamander, found only in Mexico, remains a child even when it grows up. Its fin, that resembles a tadpole's, and external gills which it had as a larva pass on into adulthood. Unlike most other salamanders, it lives only in water.

Axolotl

NOTING THE NEWT

Newts are salamanders who usually live more of their adult lives in water compared to other salamanders and have flatter tails. They are found in moist woody areas of North America, Europe and Asia.

Protective Poison

The innocent-looking red spotted newt is not as innocent as it seems. It shows its bright colours to warn predators about its poisonous skin. True to itself, it does secrete poison when it's threatened or injured. Still, this is the most common pet newt. A really bad one is the rough skinned newt, who has enough poison to kill an adult human. Native Americans in the Pacific Northwest even use it to poison their enemies!

Warty yet Handsome

You would have seen really smooth and handsome princes in fairy tales. But even though the warty newt is covered with small bumps, their males in the mating season develop a smart crest along their backs which makes them look charming. And that is why it is also known as the great crested newt. Whoever said a person with warts cannot be Prince Charming?

New(t) Love!

A male newt works really hard to impress a female by showing off his brightly coloured skin.